Art as Alchemy

An Inside View of the Transformational Process

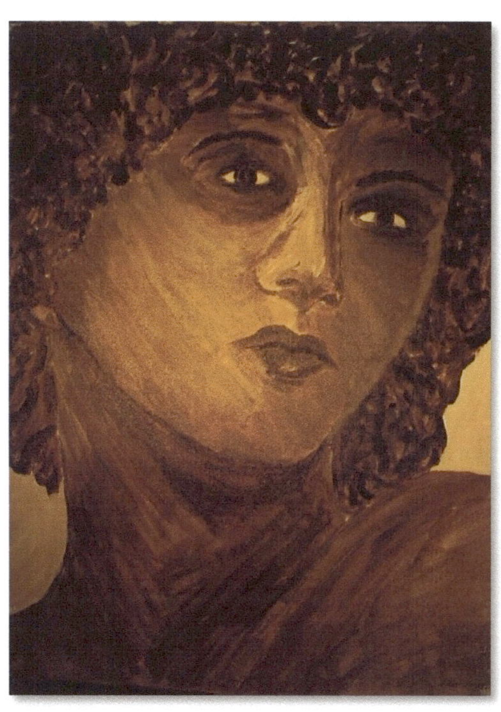

Veronica C. Wanchena

(Gabriel Orion Marie)

For Catherine Marin and Christine Muraski

These amazing women are two of my nieces. They contributed very directly to this book, by participating in its original creation as a presentation that I gave to professionals and students in the field of Art Therapy.

I dedicate *Art as Alchemy* to them with immense gratitude for their wholehearted support of me as I openly share my story and my message with the world.

I love them as much as I know how to love.

Table of Contents

Introduction

I want to simply preface my book with a very short biography ... I was sexually abused and physically and psychologically tortured throughout my childhood. I was used for child pornography and sold as a child prostitute for about 4 years. Those years of sustained terror and violence shattered my psyche. Survival came at the price of insanity. Abuse riddled my body with sexually transmitted diseases and inflated it with layers of anguish-filled fat cells.

It also unleashed in my soul every possible drop of courage, tenacity and desire to survive. My father, who was my primary abuser, died when I was 16 years old.

At 18 I ran away to Canada and joined a religious group that was like a commune in many ways. There I hid and survived, stumbled and strove. In spite of the deep dysfunctions and abuses that were also present there, it kept me alive. Fear of damnation and a pull toward suicide haunted me relentlessly. I managed to live what appeared to most people as a very intense and anxiety-ridden life, but no one really knew the depths of what I was carrying inside of me.

After 24 years in the group, I suffered a horrendous, violent, drunken assault from another member, which shattered the very wobbly psychic structure I had built over the years. Due to that assault, coupled with one of the sexually transmitted diseases being out of remission and my being deathly ill, I was reduced to a frozen heap of shattered humanity.

Consequently, the community was required to pay for me to receive professional help as a form of victim services. With the guidance of a kind and wise friend outside the community who believed in me, I was able to find a therapist that I would be able to trust. Dr. A. was a wise and well-seasoned psychologist working in Canada where I was living at the time. I was so traumatized and so deep in Post-Traumatic Stress Disorder (PTSD) and Dissociative Identity Disorder (DID) that I found it almost impossible to speak. Even when I did speak, it felt hollow and shallow. That was so frustrating because more than anything else, I needed someone who would know with me, who would witness in retrospect with me at what happened to me, what it did to me. I needed someone who would help lead me out of my abyss and into the here and now, where I could build a new life.

He was not an art therapist; but he asked me one day, a couple of months into therapy, if I thought maybe I could try to draw or paint what I was feeling and remembering, since I was having so much trouble with words. It was sheer desperation that drove me to try ... and what began to pour out of me was a torrent of drawings and paintings that provided an unexpected and thrilling catharsis that I never dreamt possible.

I have recounted that therapeutic journey in my three books, *This White House, Going Sane* and *A Spectacular Dawn.*

What I want to share here is a portion of my experience, both of the abuse and of how the use of art and the therapeutic relationship were the primary means of healing and recovery. Throughout this book, I will make reference to the key elements of the therapeutic relationship I found to be most effective and helpful. Basically, I will take you on a micro version of my journey with Dr. A.

Objective

What I want to share in this book is a portion of my experience: both of the abuse and how the use of art and the therapeutic relationship were the primary means of healing and recovery.

Throughout this book, I will refer to the key elements of the therapeutic relationship I found to be most effective and helpful.

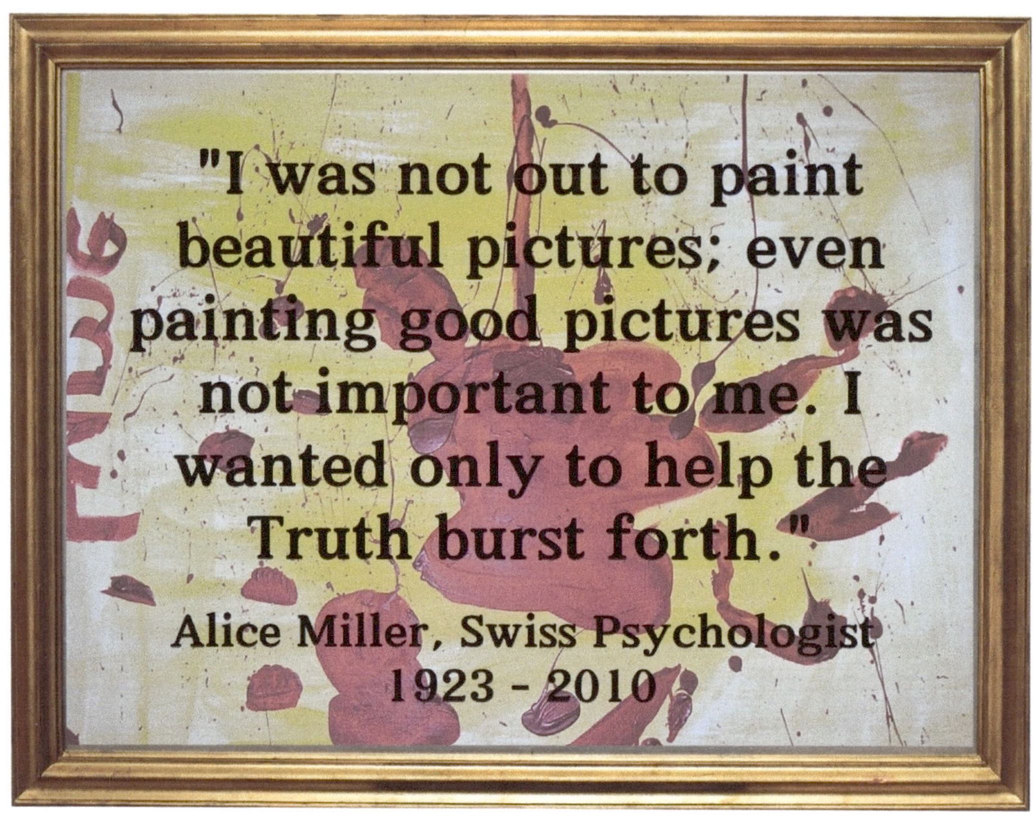

These words of Alice Miller mirrored my own intentions as I painted my story.

"Thank you, Gabriel Orion Marie, for your letter and your trust. You found the courage to confront your history and have the good fortune to do it with an enlightened witness. Even if there is much suffering on this path you are no longer in danger because you KNOW now what happened and you WANT to know. I wish you all my best and hope that my books and my paintings will help you to bear your truth and to BELIEVE in what your painting is telling you."

~ Alice Miller (From our personal correspondence 2006)

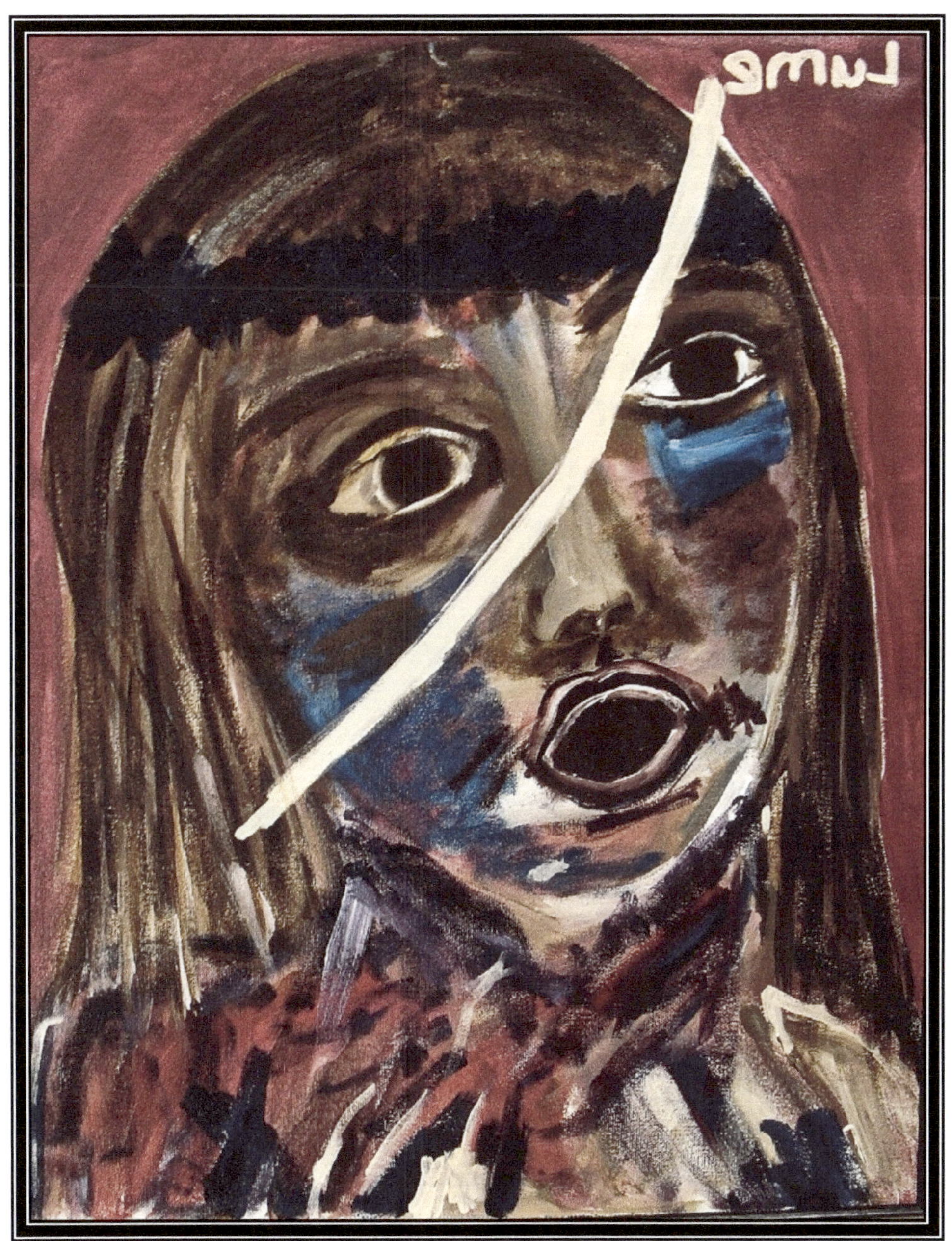

An Inside View:
Witness to the Story

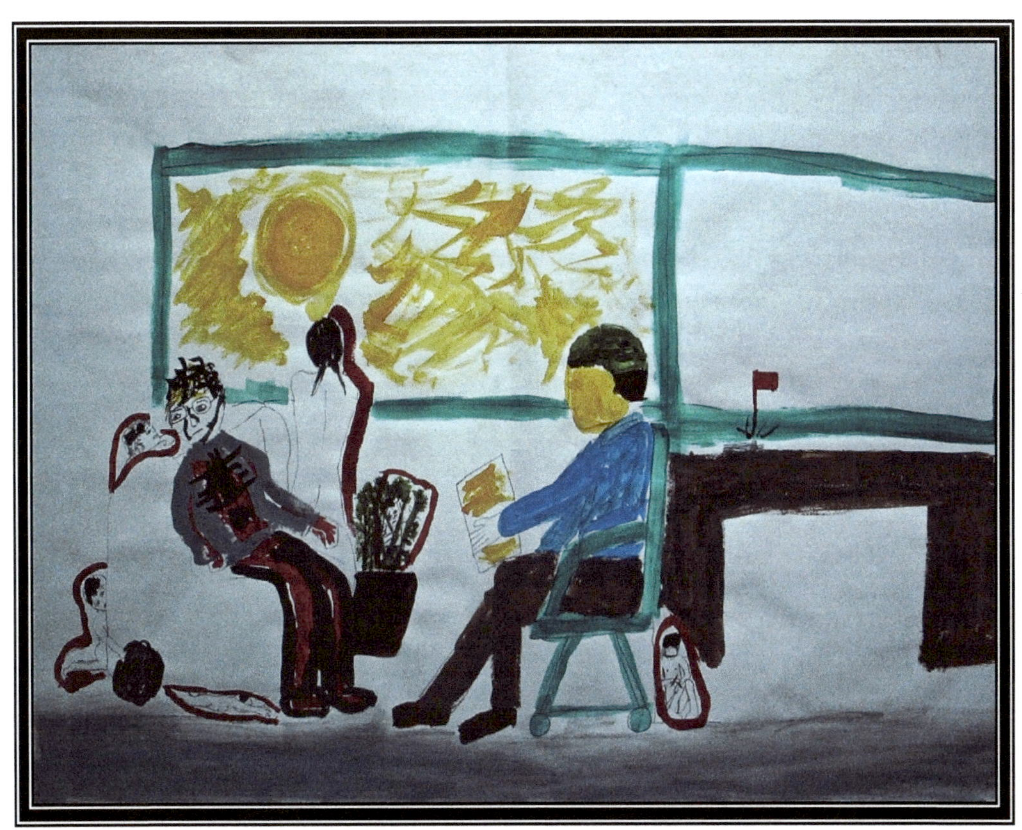

Girl at the Window

In my mind, in my soul, in my body, resided the raped and tortured child that I was. She appeared in the windows of my mind and my emotions, desperate to be rescued and comforted.

I needed a therapist who would know and believe me how bad it was.

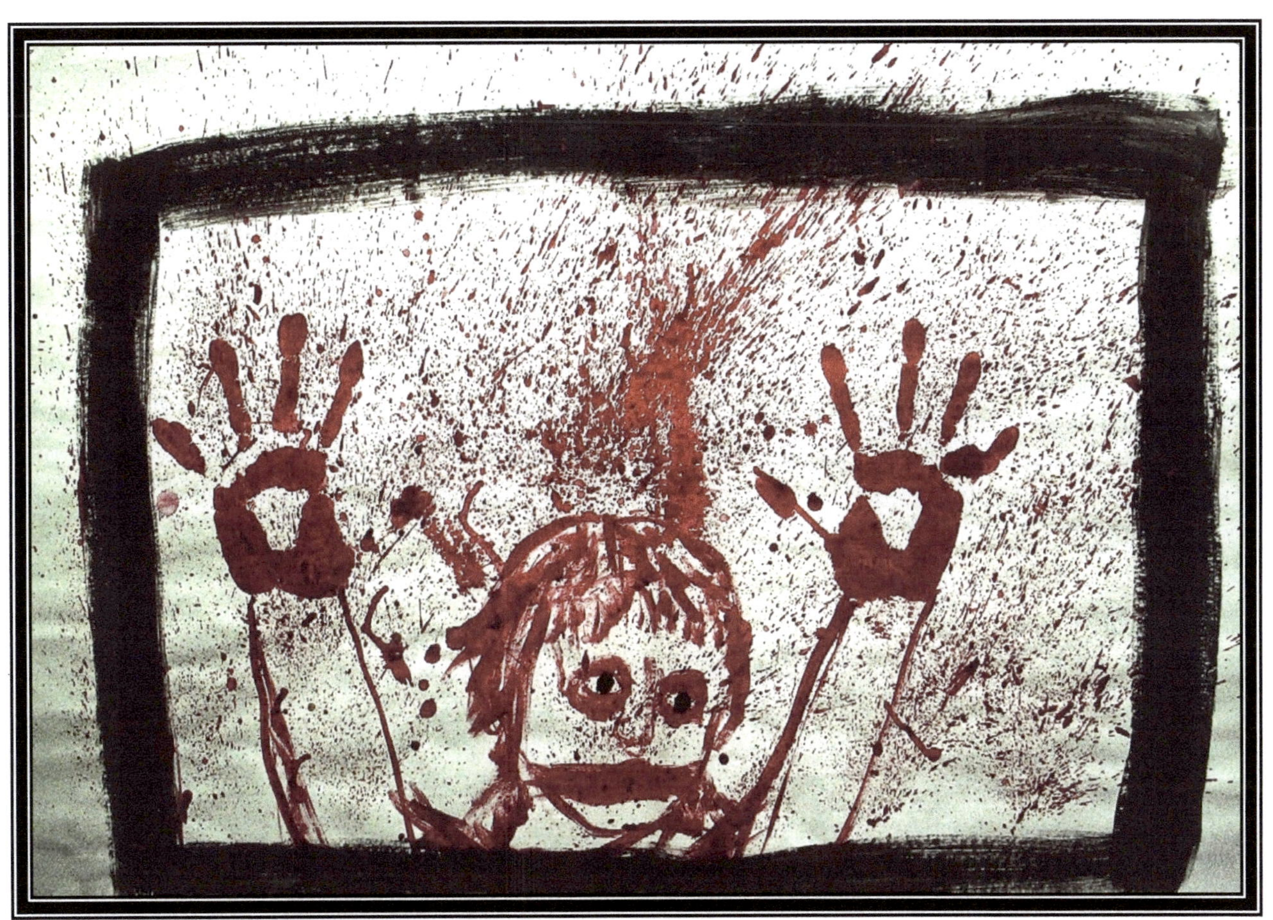

$5 Death

The child I was had been sold as a child prostitute hundreds of times. Now every monetary transaction, every kind of exchange between myself and any stranger anywhere, brought her death to the surface of my life, with all the feelings of betrayal, capture, invasion and defilement.

I needed a relationship of no debt, just clean, clear therapy. Dr. A. was there for me. Period. I was not there for him.

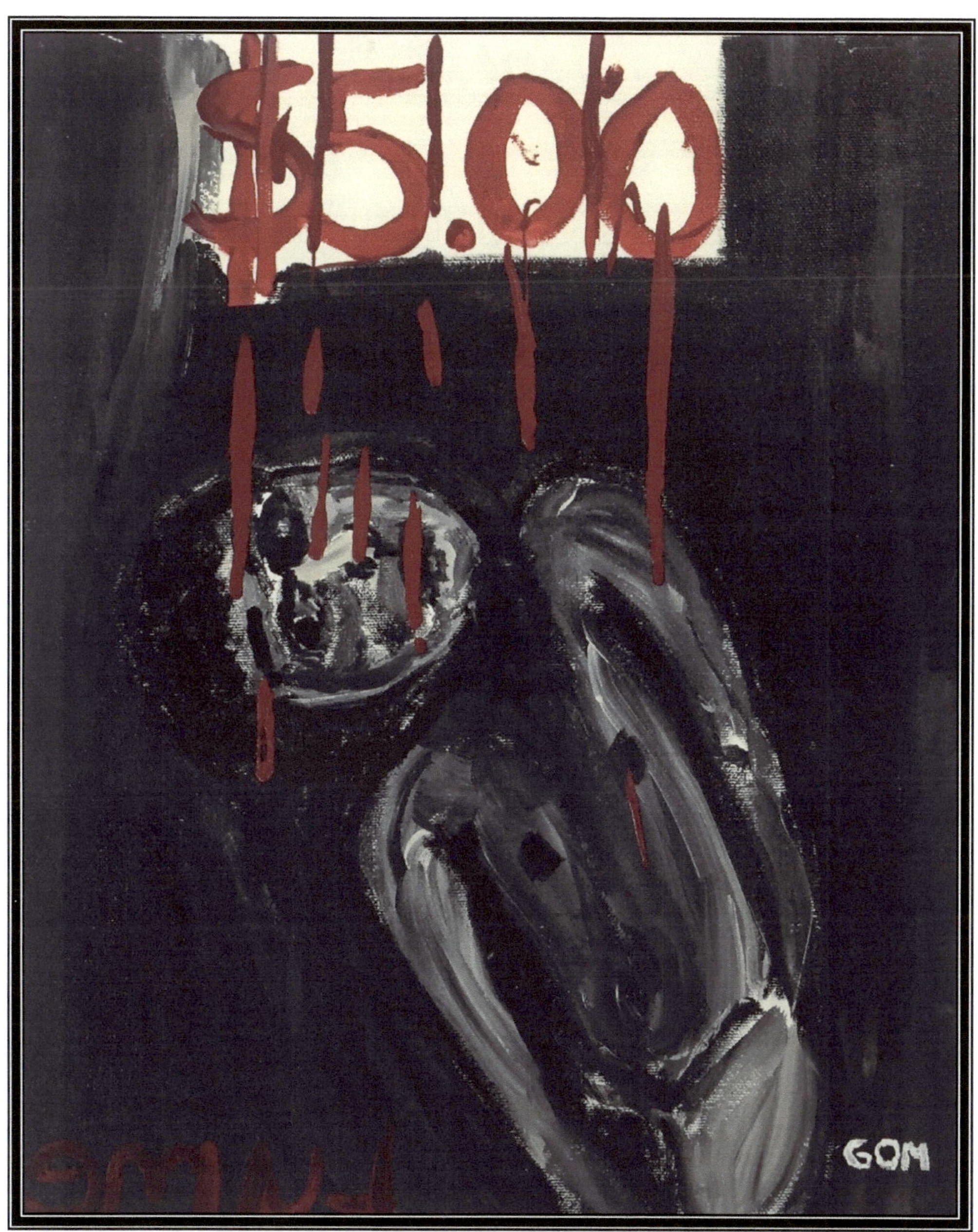

$5.00
GOM

HOLES

I had been raped several thousand times throughout infancy and childhood. This left gaping, raw holes in my sense of being, in my psyche, in my heart. The repetitive invasion of rape bored holes in me that prevented me from being able to contain or retain anything, except for the *holes* themselves.

It was the therapeutic bond that became the first layer of healing these holes because it was the first relationship from which I was finally able to trust and receive.

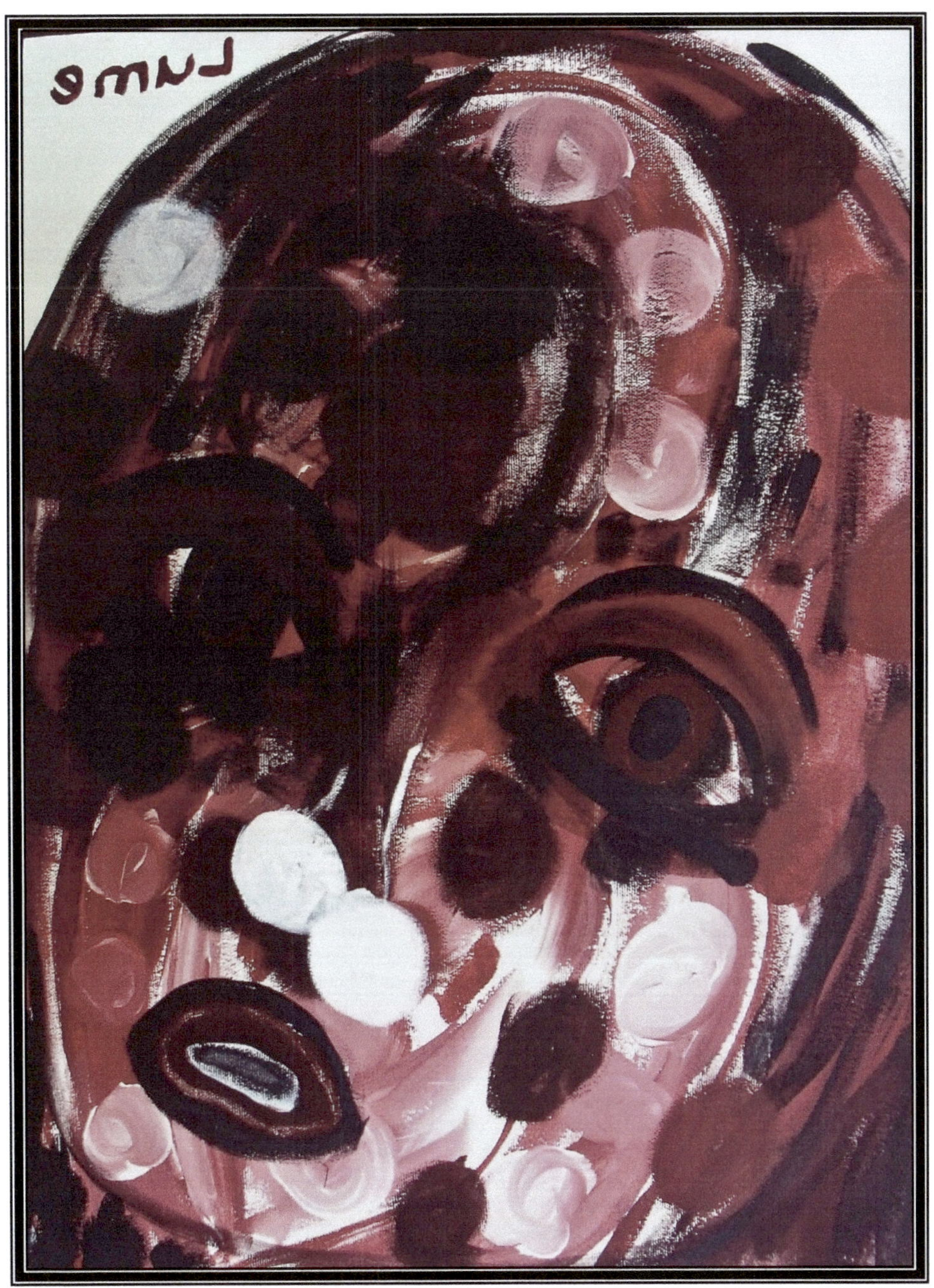

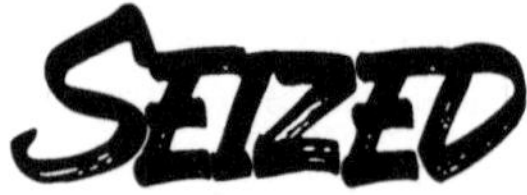Seized

My entire being, body, mind and spirit was contracted with unspeakable terror. My father pressed me against the wall, and raped me from every angle. Years later I would need a tremendous amount of trust and coaching to learn how to breathe again.

I needed prolonged and sustained patience, kindness and consistency from Dr. A. in order to even begin to let any part of my body or my mind relax, even for a short period of time.

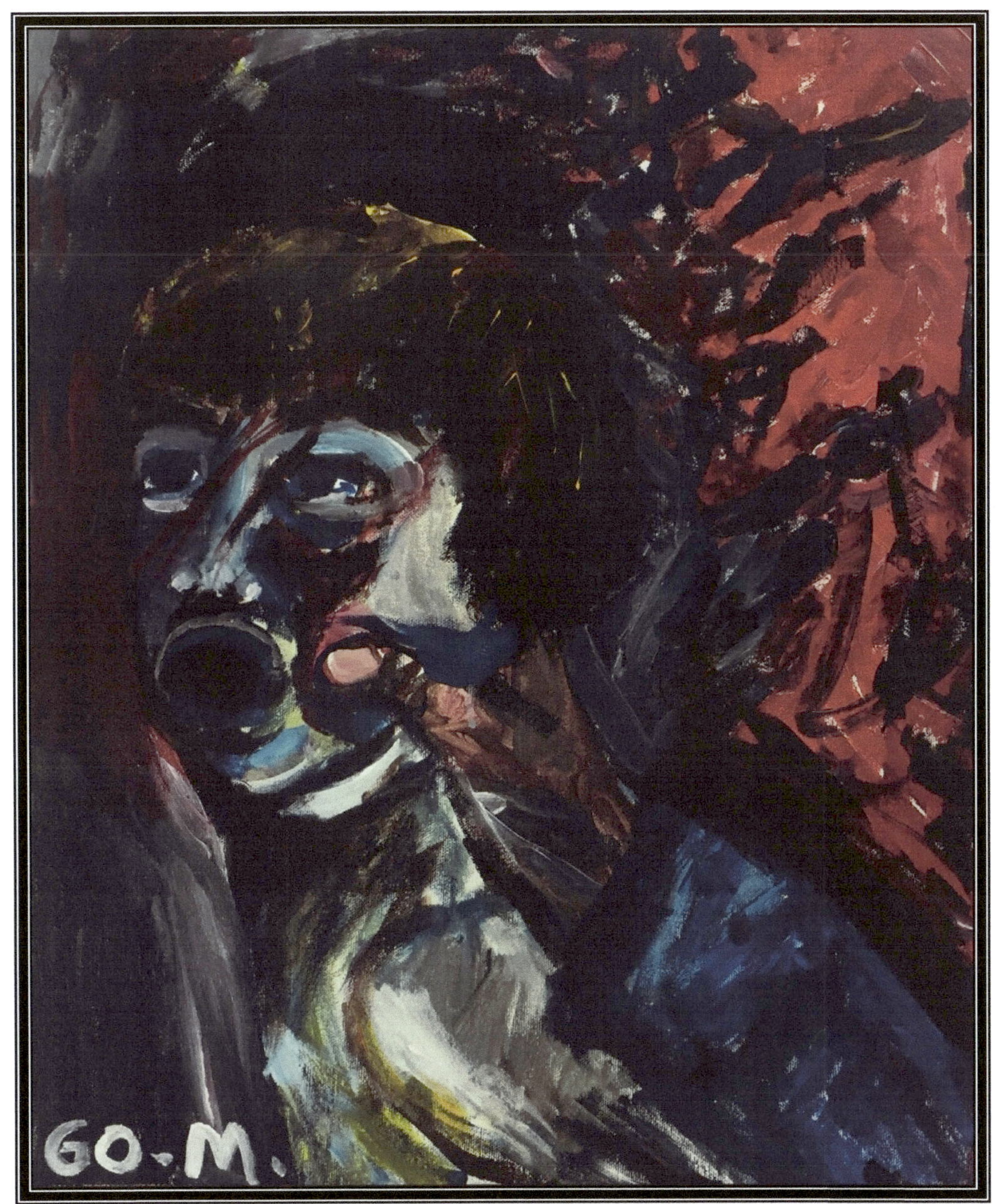

GO.M.

Segreto Oscuro (Dark Secret)

The Dark Secrets were the torture and brainwashing sessions that happened in the garage or in the hotel rooms. I have detailed them in my books.

In order to provide an arena of the most trustworthy safety where I could reveal the Darkest Secrets of torture and brainwashing, I needed to know that Dr. A. was strong, that he was safe within himself and that my story would not harm him. Now that I had found and begun to trust a therapist, the greatest danger was that my story would poison him, harm him. That was a threat with which my torturers had left me. Many victims fear that their pain will harm, soil or poison the very people whom they need to disclose it to.

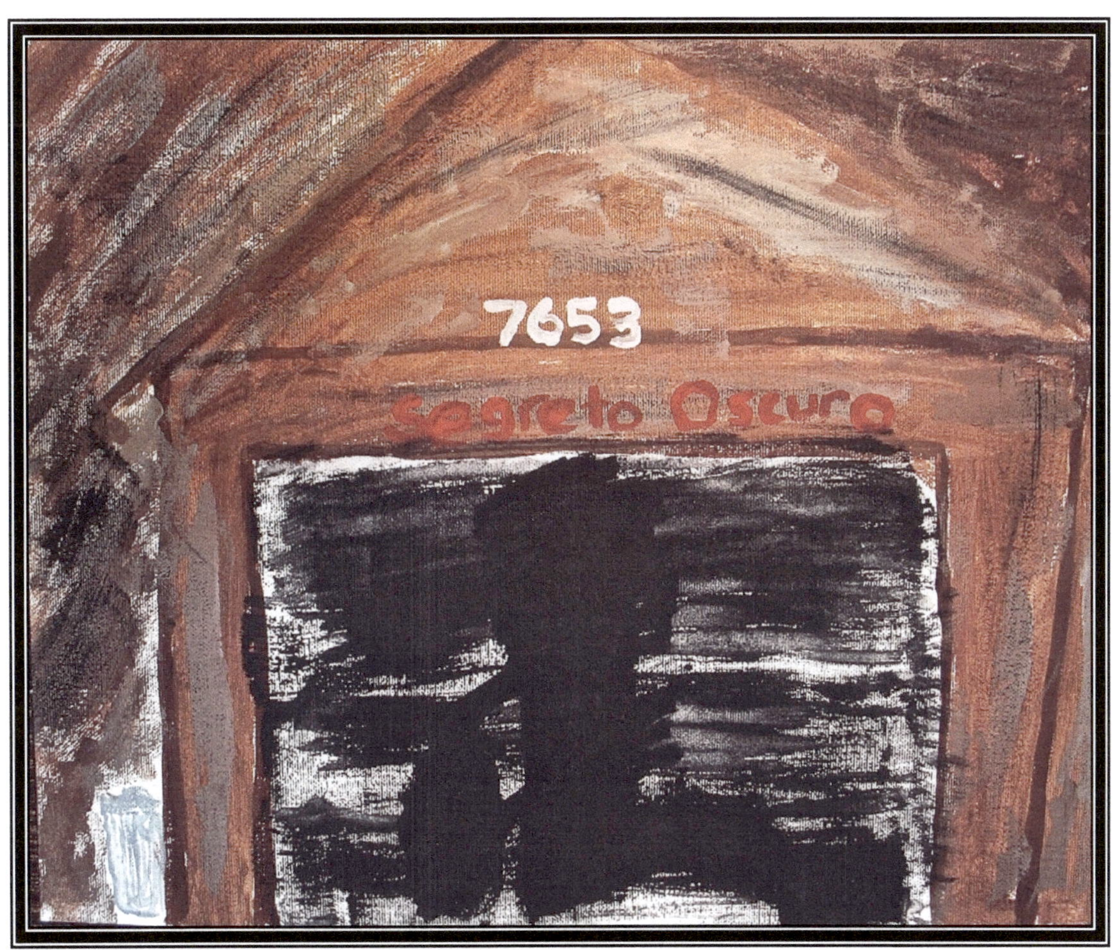

7653
Segreto Oscuro

Stages of the Burden

When I arrived at Dr. A.'s office for the first time, I was 44 years old. I had collapsed under the last assault. But I needed to process all the *Stages of the Burden* with him.

It required a commitment from both Dr. A. and me that we would leave no stone unturned and that I would be in therapy for as long as necessary. I knew that I would not survive unless I got deep, thorough healing. Symptom management would no longer suffice.

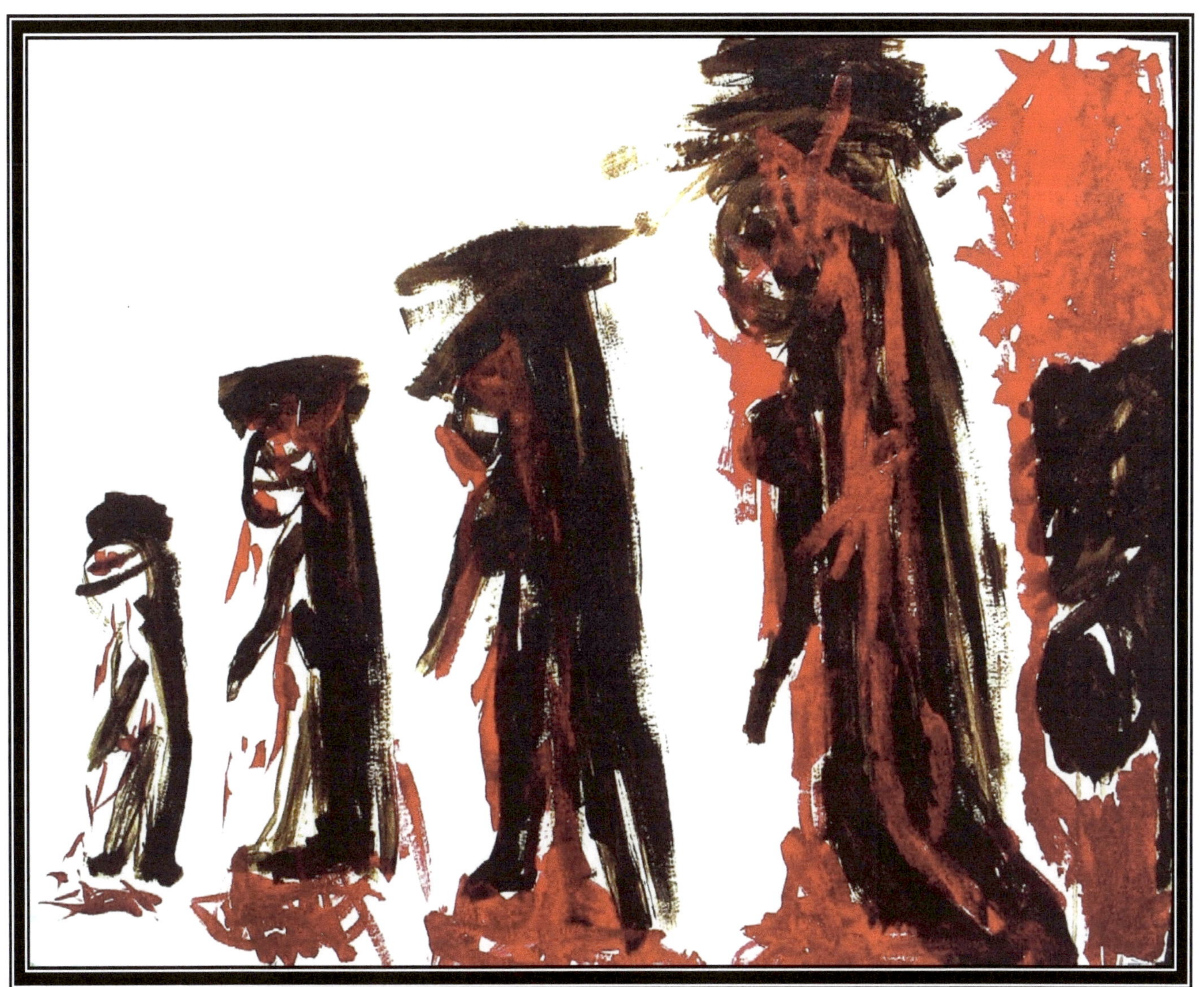

Solo

My story only happened to me. I was all alone in it and although I needed Dr. A. as a Witness to my recounting, my reliving of it. It was *my* story. The only way I could get the freedom and healing I wanted was by owning and claiming the whole story as mine.

I needed Dr. A. to not work out his stuff through my story, at least not in my presence. He constantly held up the mirror of truth that my life only happened to me. He affirmed the solitary journey this was, and yet stood faithfully as my personal Witness.

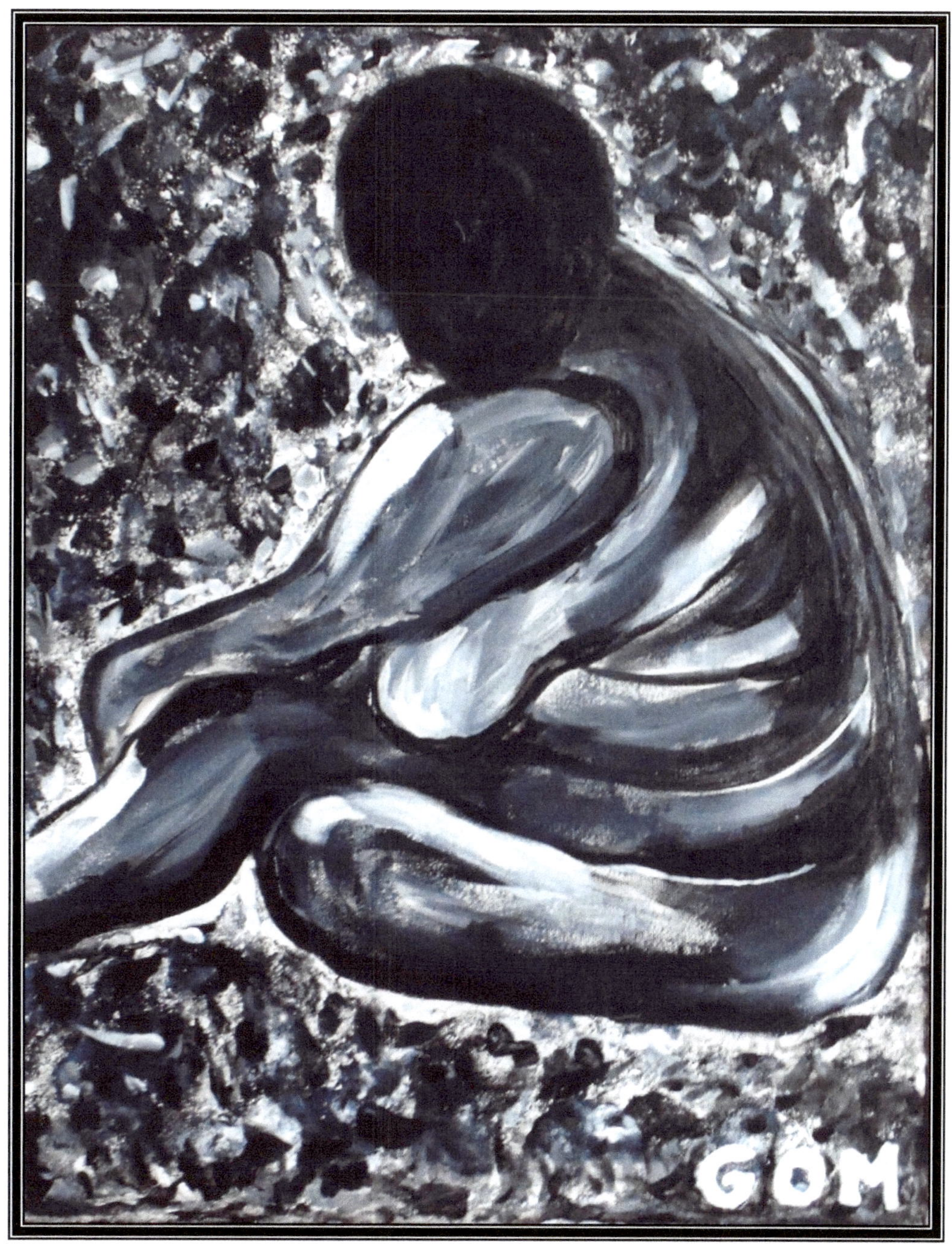

GOM

Art as Alchemy: Witness to the Fire

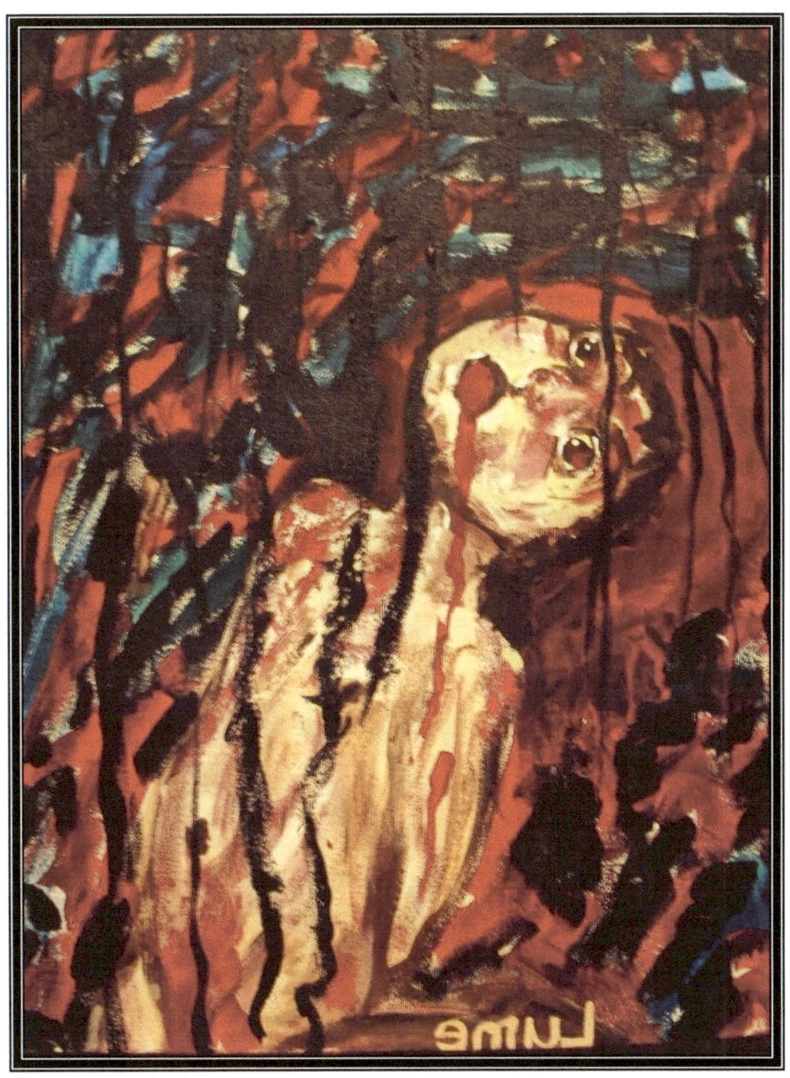

Diving Into the Abyss

The healing process required that I dive down deep into the abyss of the wounds, in order to bring everything into the light and air for healing.

I could only make the dive once I had established a foundation of trust in the therapeutic relationship. I tested Dr. A.'s trustworthiness repeatedly, especially in the first few years of our work together and that, too, was a necessary part of the process. Trusting Dr. A. and diving deep were profoundly connected.

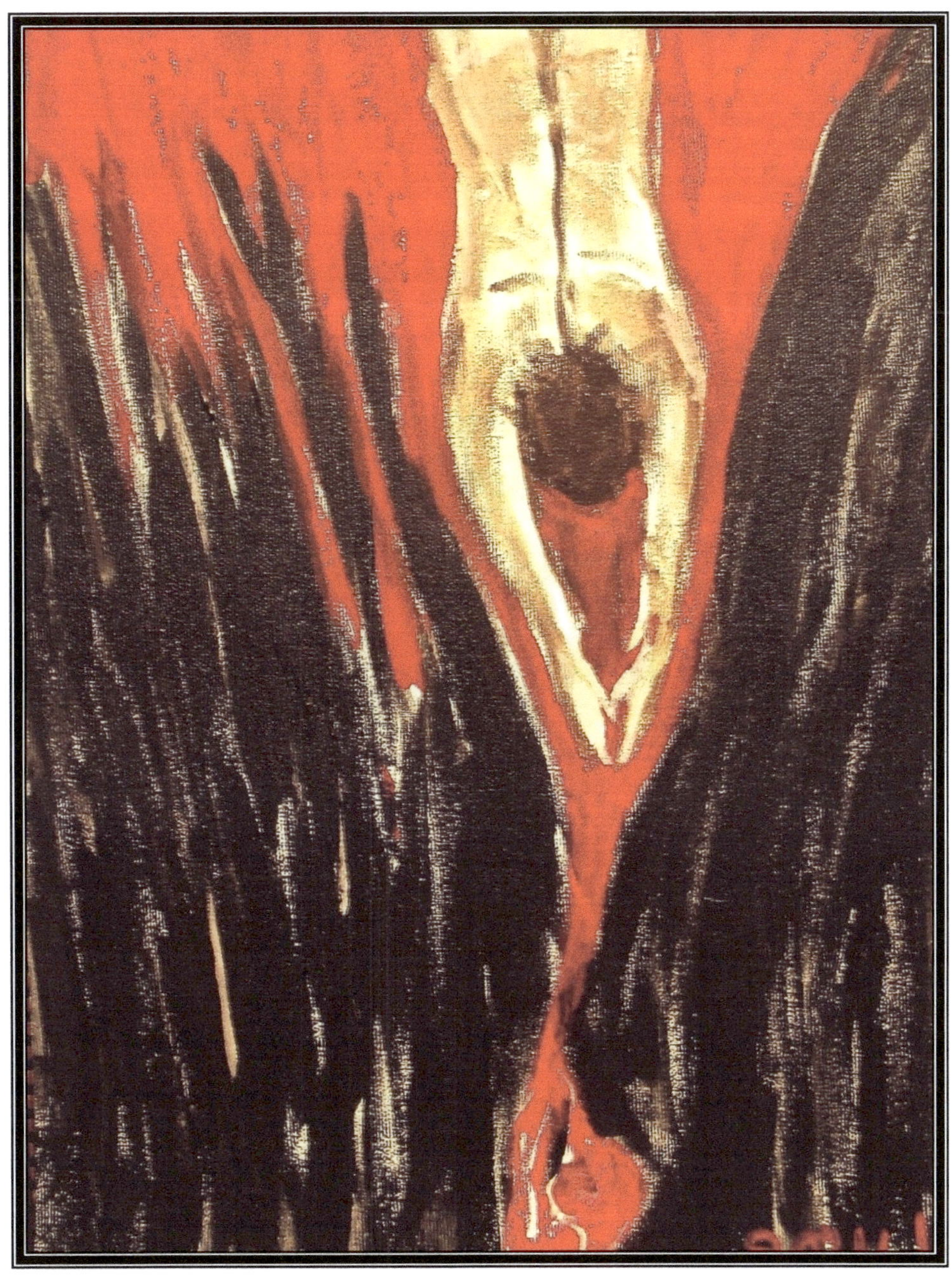

Sensation Overload

In the abyss of the wounds I encountered, I re-experienced and brought to the surface the repressed and suppressed sensations of my years of physical, emotional and psychological torture and violence.

This was absolutely necessary. I needed Dr. A. not to mitigate, not to assuage, not to shrink back from what I brought up. I needed him to witness the fire of my anguish, to encourage me to feel and embrace every drop of it, without expressing much emotion himself. He knew that my healing required my claiming of it all, in order to release it.

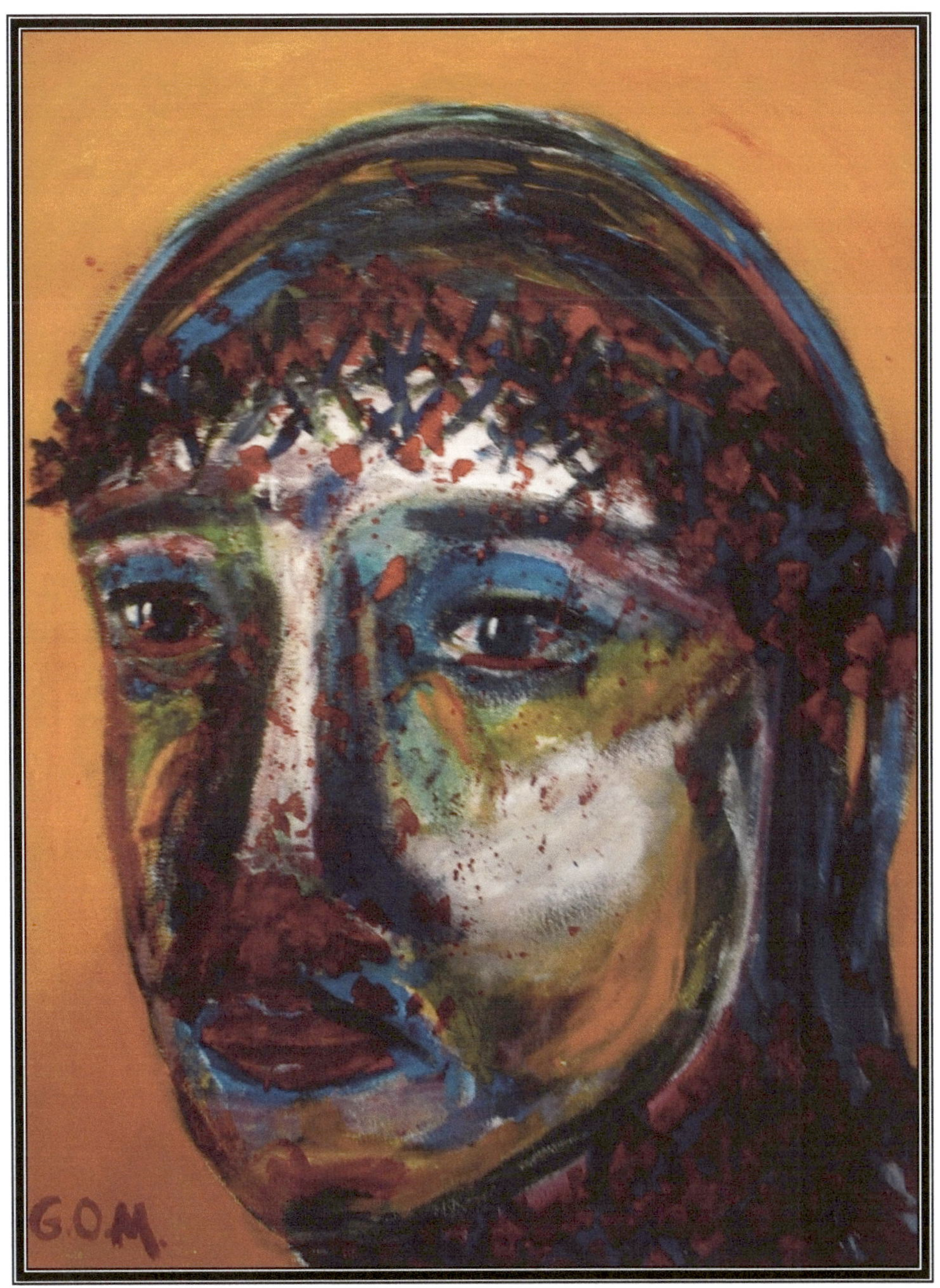
G.O.M.

Comatose Senses

Between many sessions, between many layers of my inner work, there was this coma ... where I felt numb and far, far, away. This feeling of being in a coma was the consequence of years of sensation overload. I continually cycled between overload and coma during my childhood and again during my therapeutic process.

I needed to embrace this numb experience as much I as I needed to embrace the sensations. The absence of feeling is itself a deep wound. Dr. A.'s acceptance of me, in whatever state I was in, mirrored for me the kind of self-acceptance I needed to persevere in the process and to find true healing.

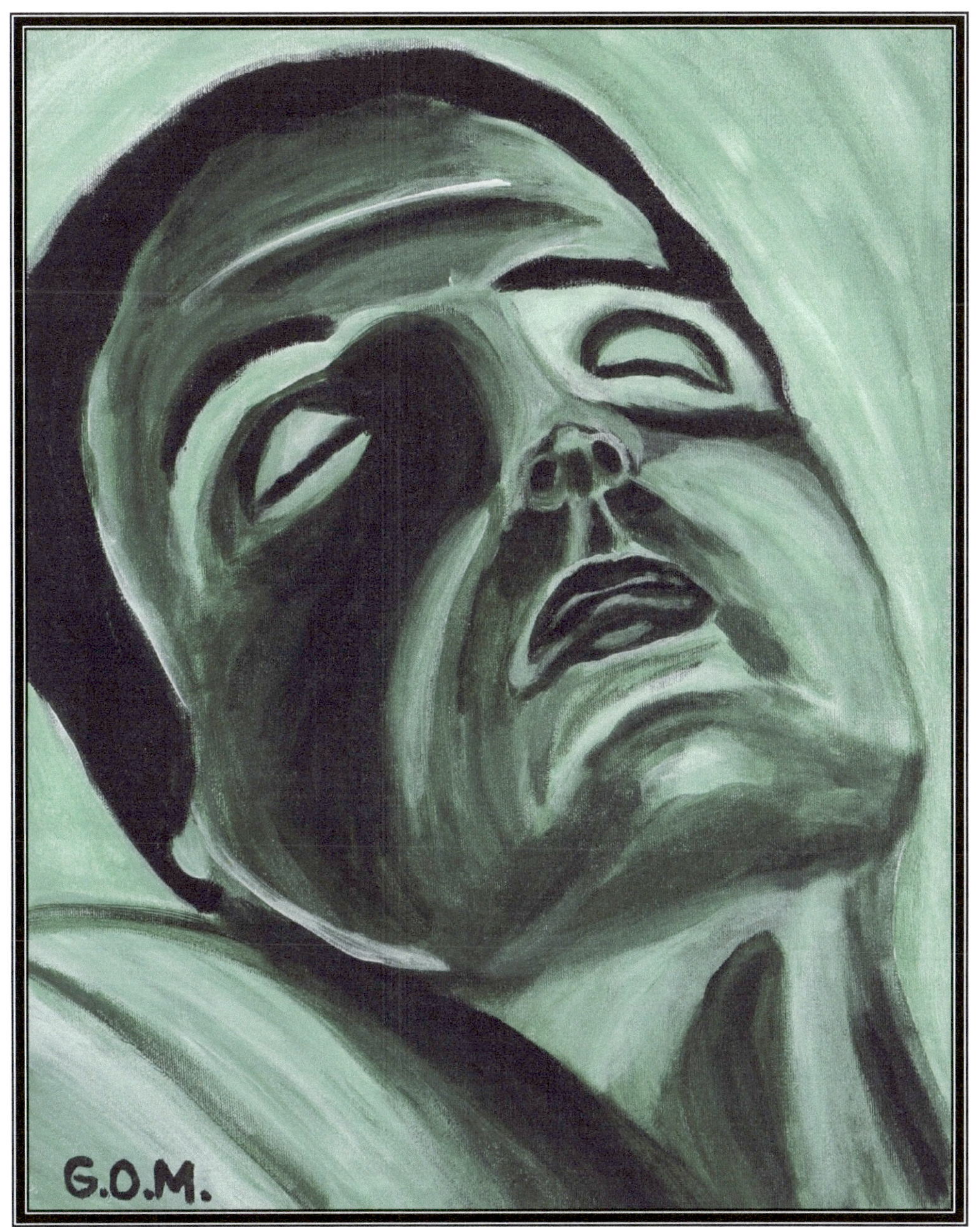
G.O.M.

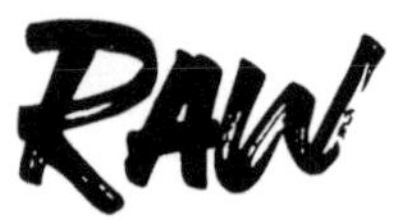

This is how I often felt during my years in therapy. Completely, emotionally and psychically raw, to the point where the slightest trigger literally sent shockwaves of hot pain through my body and mind.

I needed my boundaries respected on all counts, and at all times by Dr. A. I needed to know that being so raw in his presence would be met with compassion and respectful emotional space. I needed him to always allow me to set the pace, according to my level of raw vulnerability each day, each week.

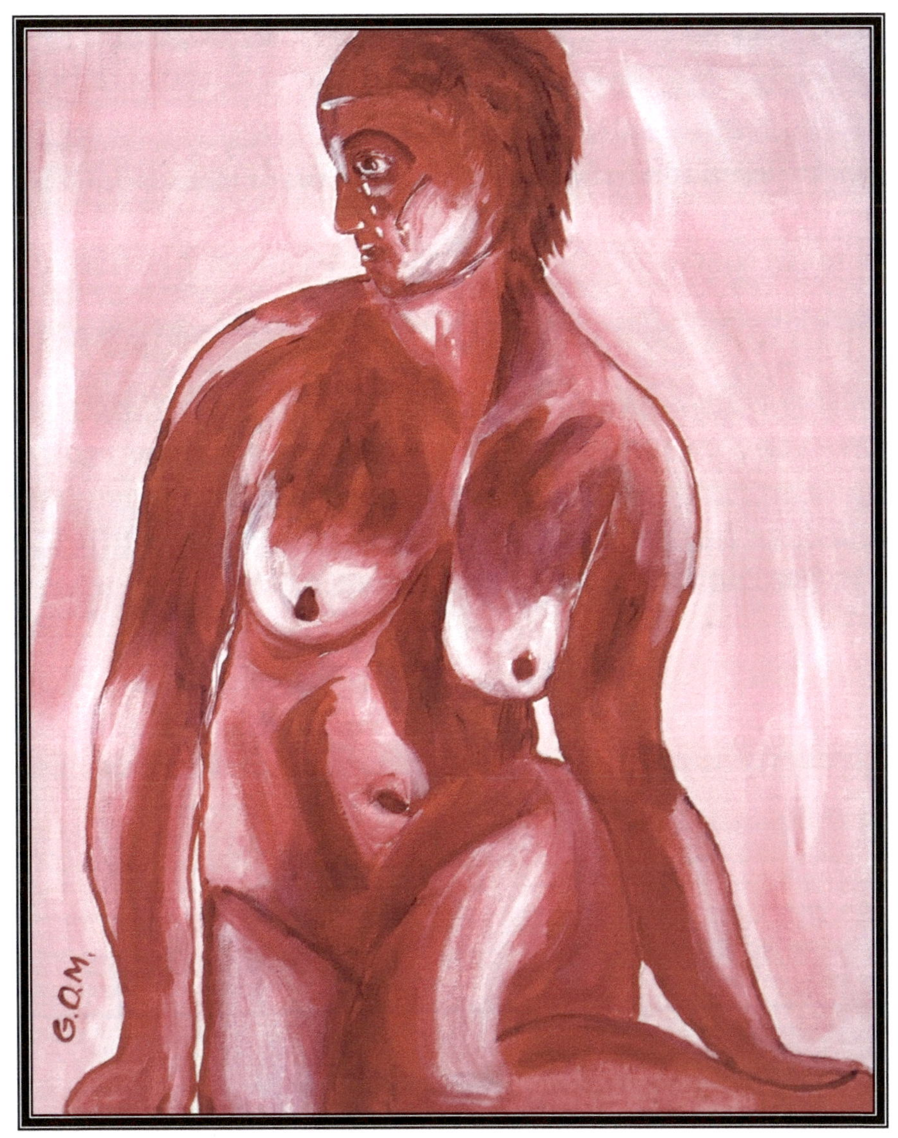

G.O.M.

Boy Knocked Over

My father forced me *to be a boy* for him, on demand. This sadistic and brainwashing abuse drove me deeply insane. I learned to create many personas over the years to meet his demands. It knocked me over inside and I often lost any sense of reality regarding my own gender, age, and orientation to time and place.

I needed Dr. A. to be unmoved and hold very still as I painted and processed out loud all the wounds and horrors of torture that were embedded in the gender question. He needed to accept me, however I presented myself at each session, until through the fire, I melded and found that it was all Me.

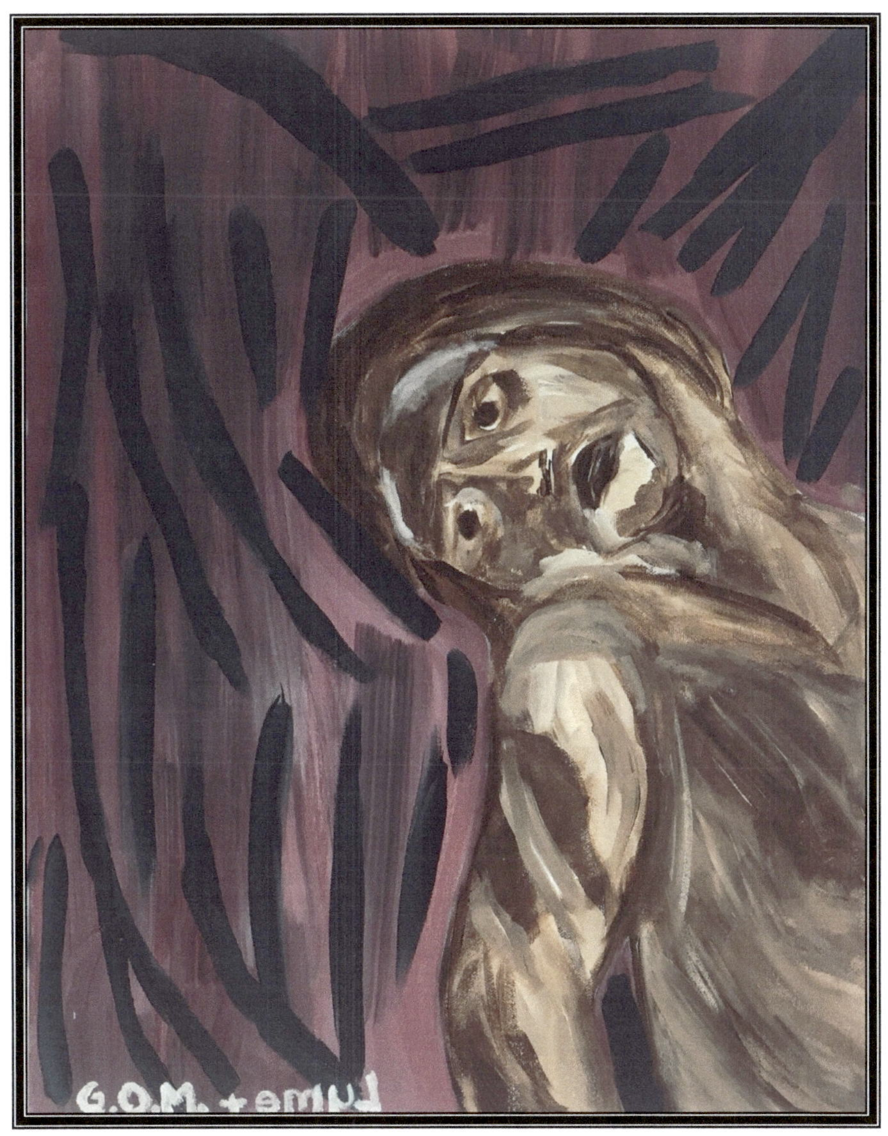

Girl at the Well

Part of me became very wise and very deep, very early on. This painting revealed the part of me that doubted the therapeutic process, doubted Dr. A. She questioned him, and she challenged him often. She had an old soul, but a child's heart.

Dr. A. let me challenge him, though in all of our communications we had simple, basic rules of respect. Each session I was required to give my word to him, the one commitment of no harm to myself or others.

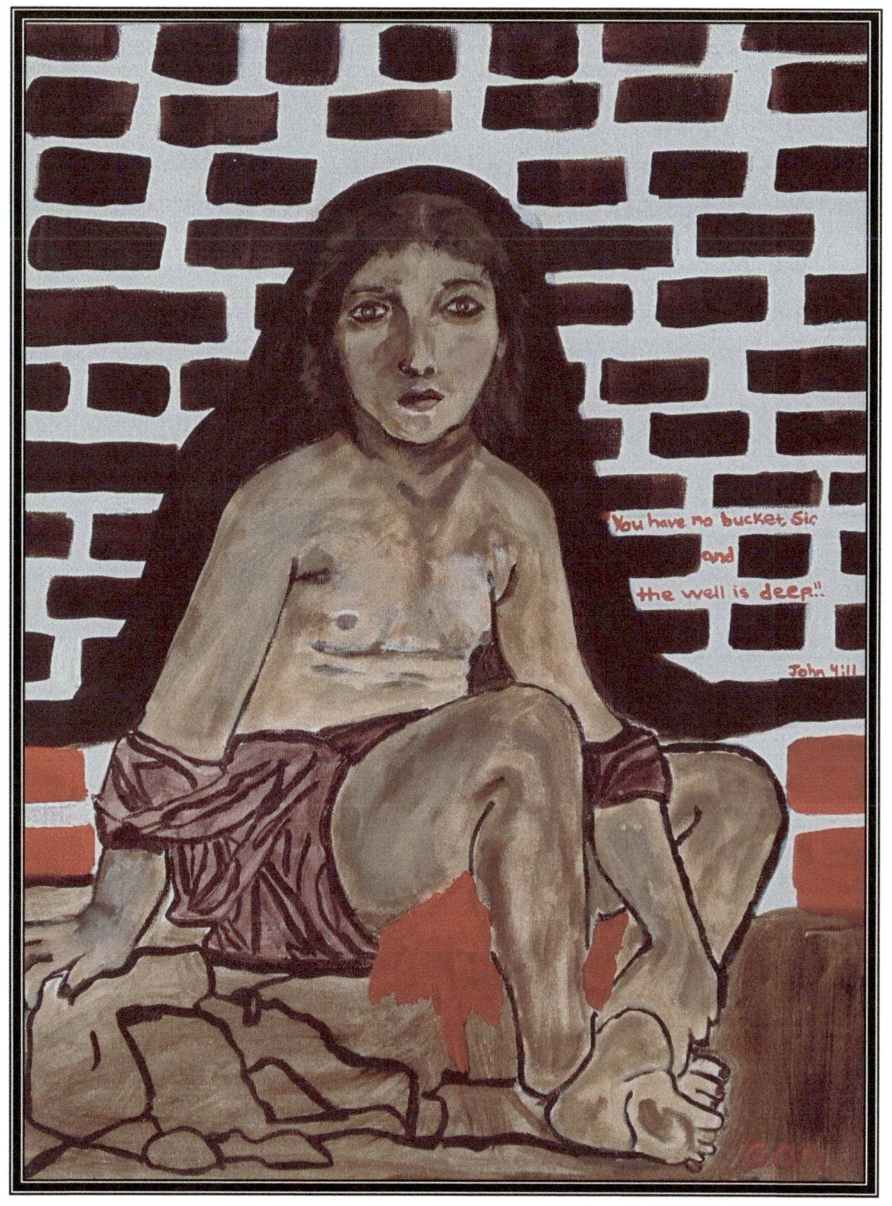

You have no bucket Sir
and
the well is deep.!!
John 4:11

UNBIND HIM

Deep in the core of my heart, part of me was imprisoned, chained and despairing. I had been driven insane, and I did not know who I was, male or female, child or adult.

Healing required that I experience this grief-laden place, and through my own acceptance of all that bound me, the chains gradually melted in the fire of the journey. I needed Dr. A. to witness the prison and the chains, but to leave the unbinding to my own inner wisdom, lest I become a victim of a miracle, still dependent on something outside of me for rescue.

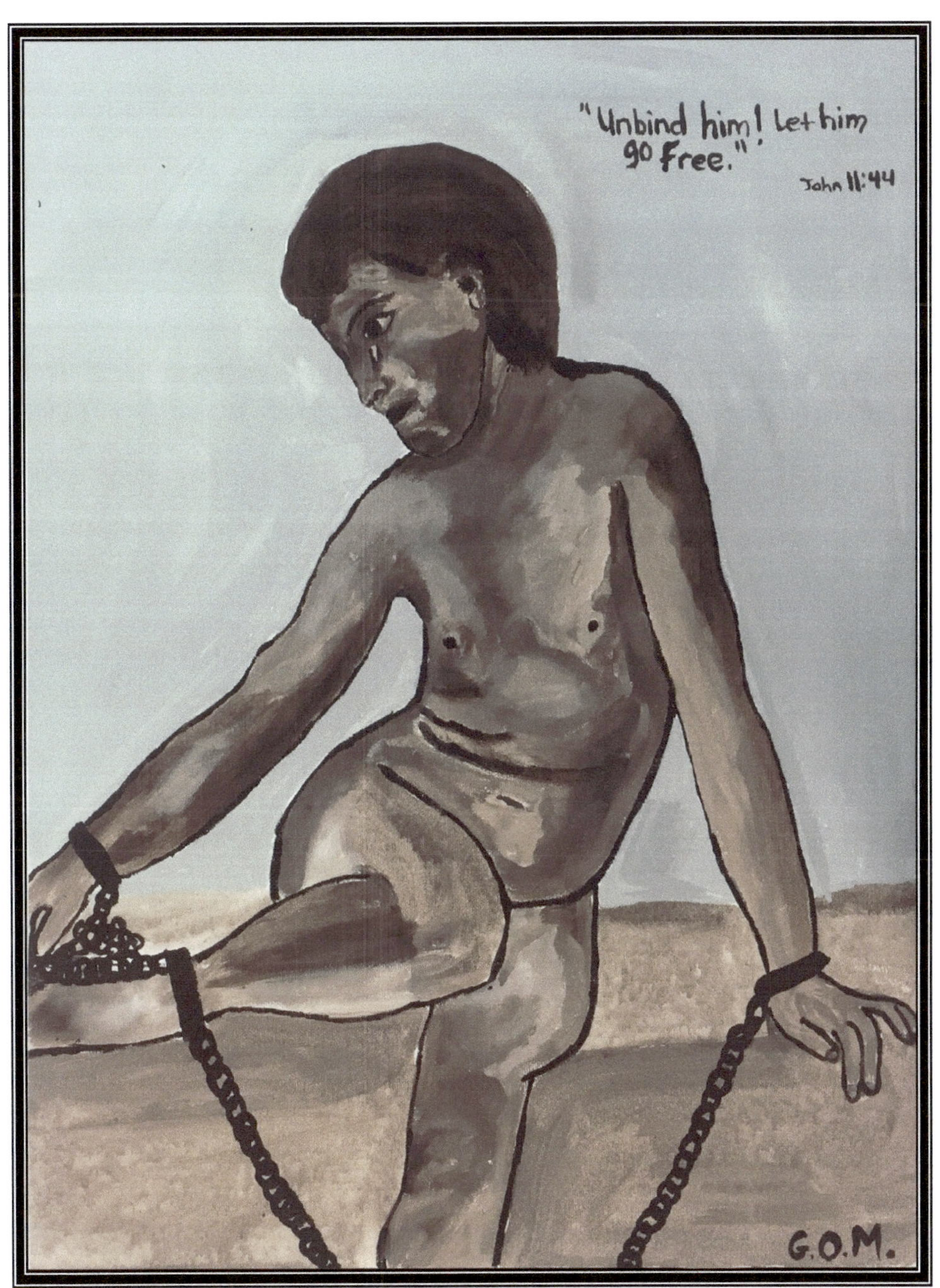
"Unbind him! Let him
go free."
John 11:44
G.O.M.

Transformation: Witness to and Mirror the Gold

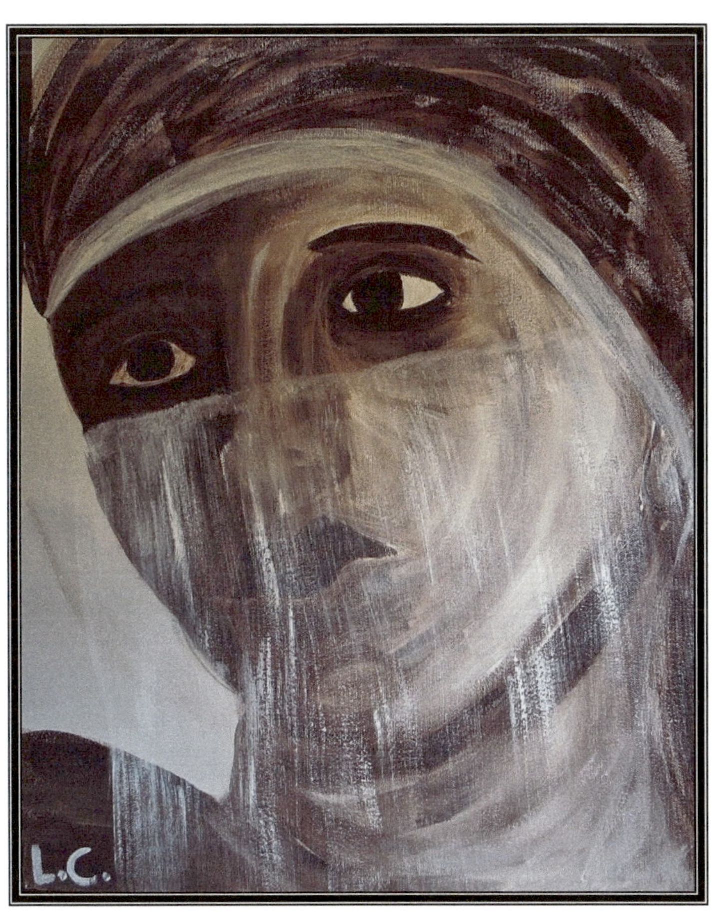

Considering

One evening, several years into therapy, I had a moment of deep considering, an objective ah-ha moment, a birds-eye view of what I was doing in therapy. I saw the phenomenal effort and courage this thorough healing process was requiring of me and I knew I was only about a third of the way through ... I had to consider if I could continue.

Throughout the years I needed Dr. A. to quietly but steadily witness to the capacity that I was exhibiting throughout the process, as a way of encouraging me. The fact that he never once doubted my ability to heal, that he did not need to consider if I had what it took, was crucial for me.

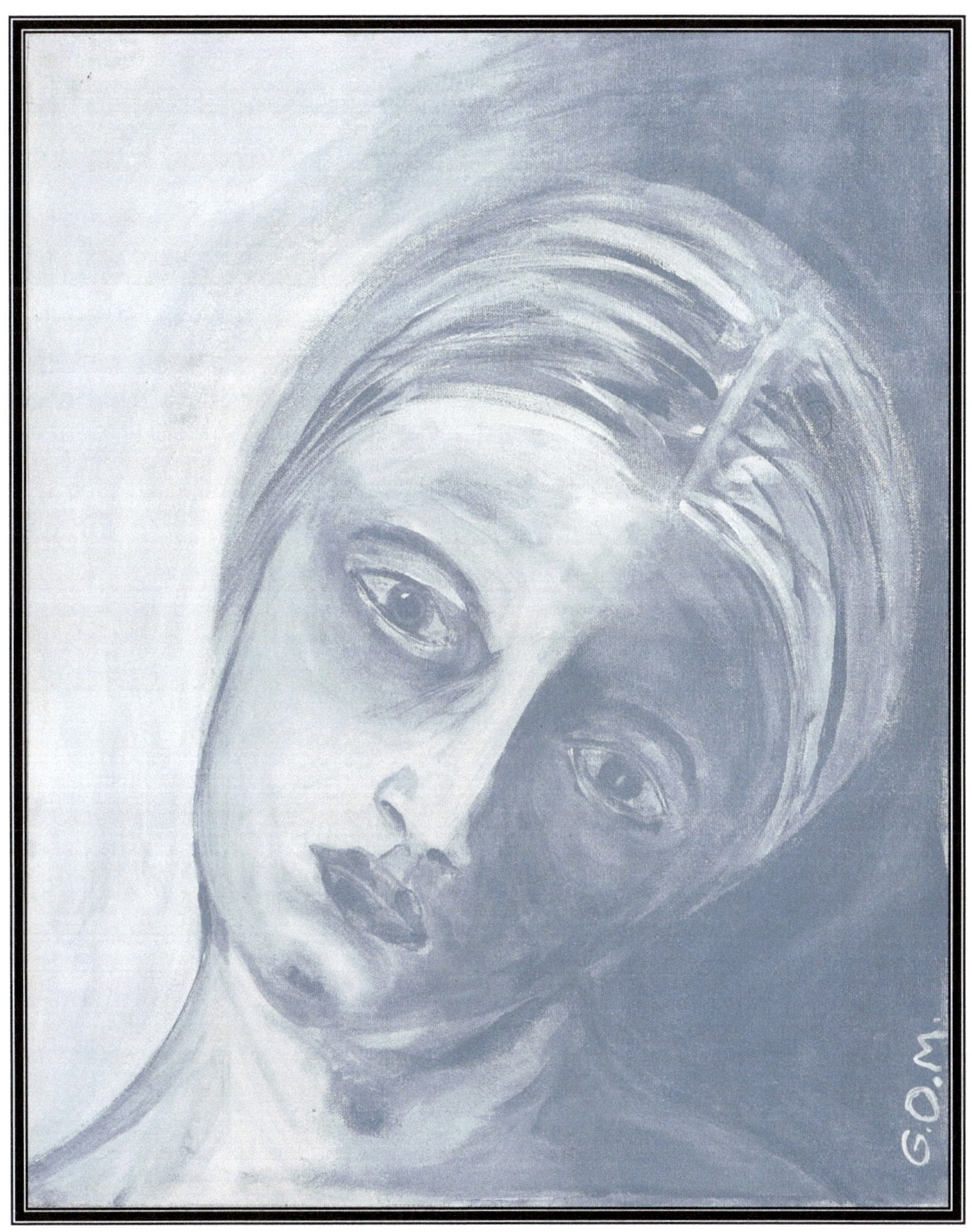

G.O.M.

Stretch Out Your Hand

In the Gospel of Matthew, Jesus says to the man with a withered hand, "Stretch out your hand". He asks the man to do precisely what he cannot do and it is in doing what he cannot do, that the man's hand is healed. That is what so much of my inner work required of me, doing what I could not do.

When the healing process called forth sanity and courage from me, it was usually when I was most anguished with mental illness and terrified out of my mind. With the steady support of my Enlightened Witness, I gradually did more and more of what I could not do. That is healing.

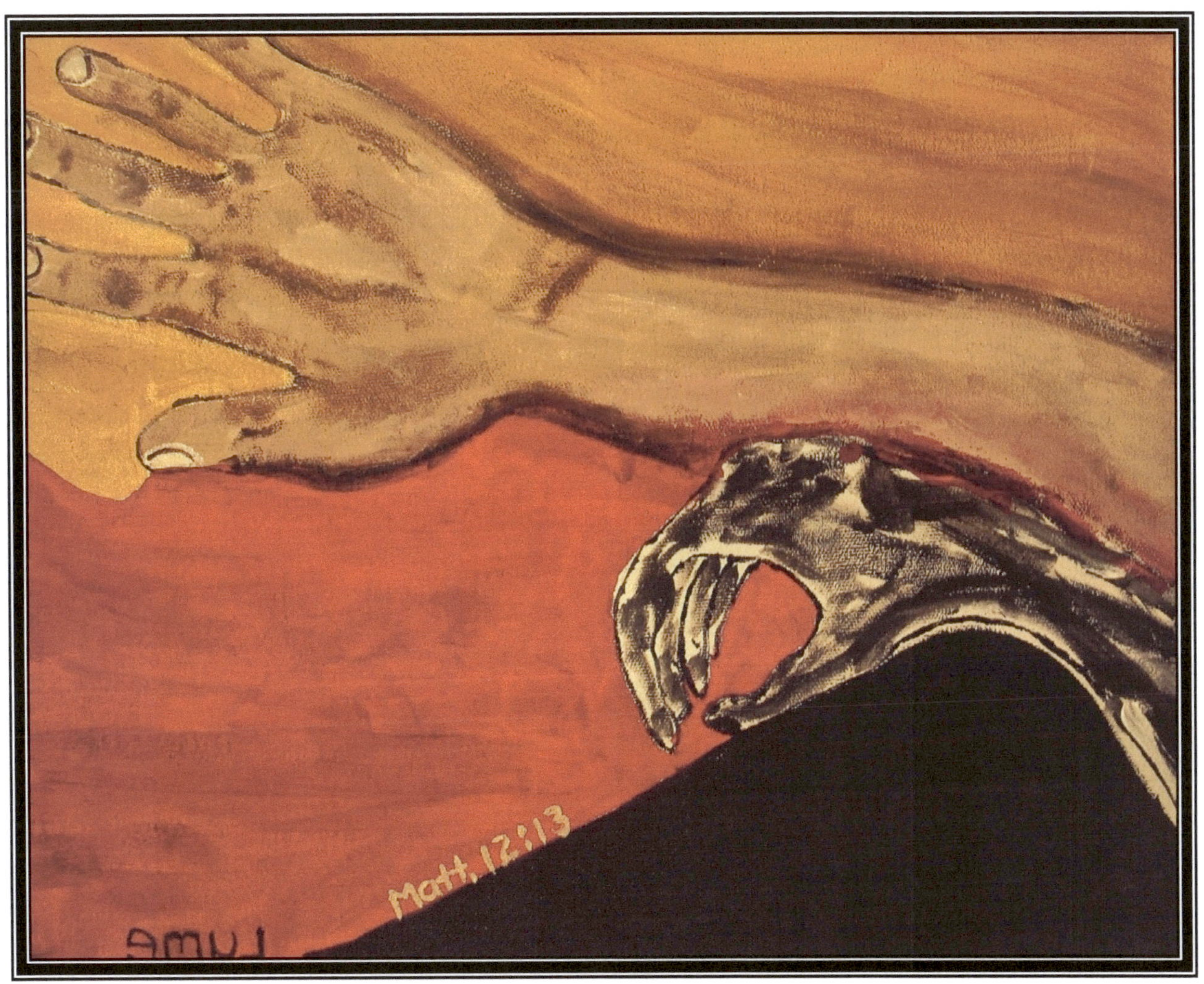
Matt. 12:13
amuI

Ave Maria

This scene is from the Passion of Christ, made into my own. At a certain point I discover the Mother that I am to the Child in me who suffered innocently and horrifically. The cement flooring was between us, yet we both knew of each other's presence. Oh, what a magnificent discovery! I am both Mother and Child. I do not need to look elsewhere.

Though I constantly aimed both positive and negative parental projections at Dr. A., he never behaved in a parental way towards me. He treated me as an equal. The only authority he exercised was requiring me to make and keep the commitment to not harm myself or others. This is what led me to find the parent within.

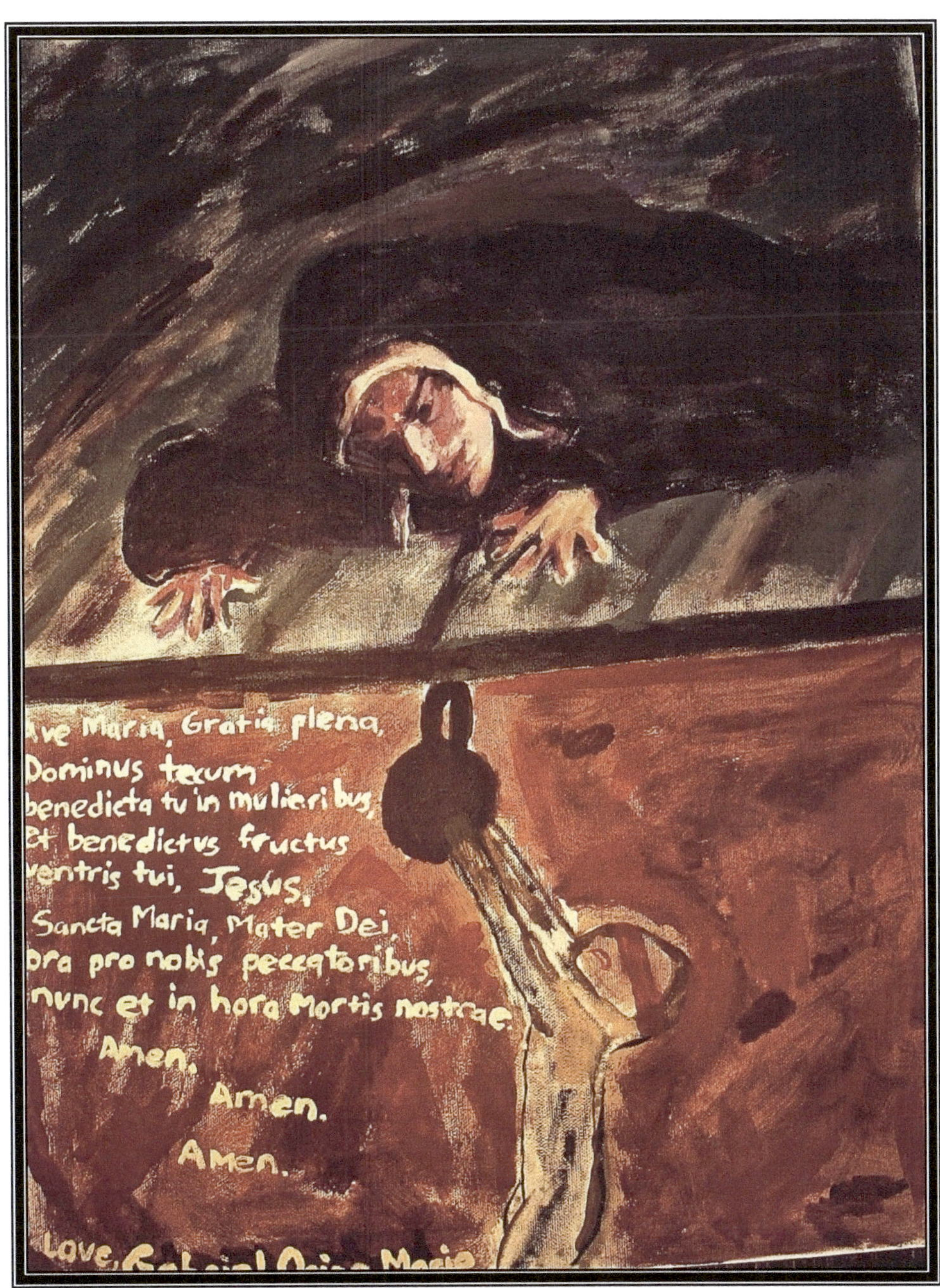
Ave Maria, Gratia plena,
Dominus tecum
benedicta tu in mulieribus,
Et benedictus fructus
ventris tui, Jesus,
Sancta Maria, Mater Dei
Ora pro nobis peccatoribus,
nunc et in hora mortis nostrae.
Amen.
Amen.
Amen.
Love, Gabriel Ơino Maria

Archangel Gabriel

From my early childhood I have had experiences of the invisible. There was an Angel, whom I came to know as Gabriel, who appeared numerous times in my lifetime and who gave me assistance and guidance when I was in the most life-threatening and soul-crushing experiences. I do not believe I would have survived my childhood without this celestial Being called Gabriel.

Regardless of what he personally believed, Dr. A. always respected my recounting of my experiences of invisible Beings. He encouraged me to trust my own experience and to explore the meaning and messages that came from dreams and visions. That quiet validation helped me as I sifted through them over the years, discovering and claiming my own relationship with both the visible and the invisible worlds.

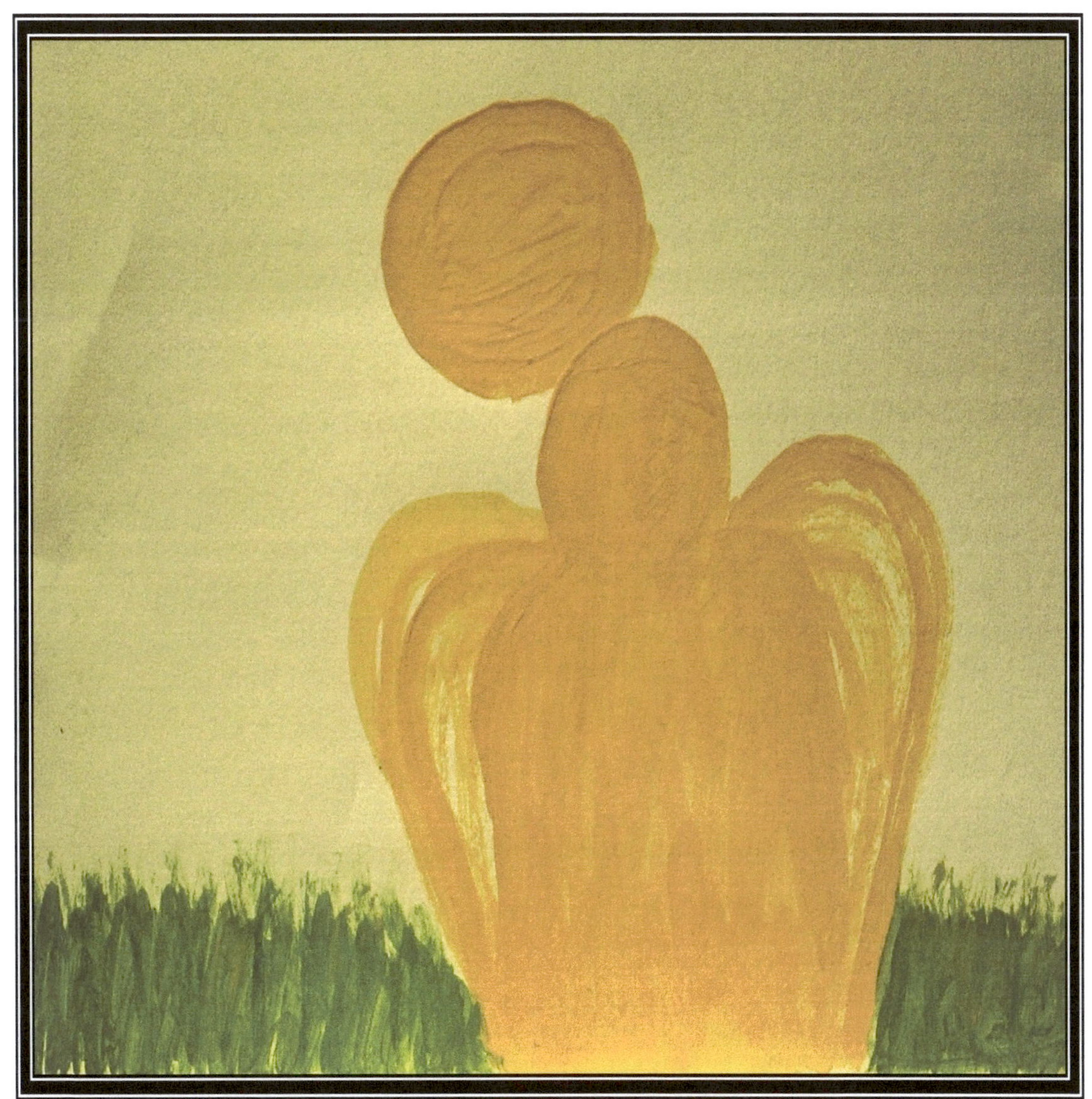

VICTORIOUS CHILD

What emerges from within as healing progress is the Victorious Mother and the Victorious Child. I am truly both. Here the Child's wounded mind is still wrapped in a bandage, but he/she is strong, powerful and alive. The mother is proud, quiet, maternal and knowing.

Here is the Gold emerging from the alchemic fire of therapy. This is the beginning of a profound self-possession and self-knowledge. This is where I laid hold of unshakable self-respect and self-support that is the goal of all therapy.

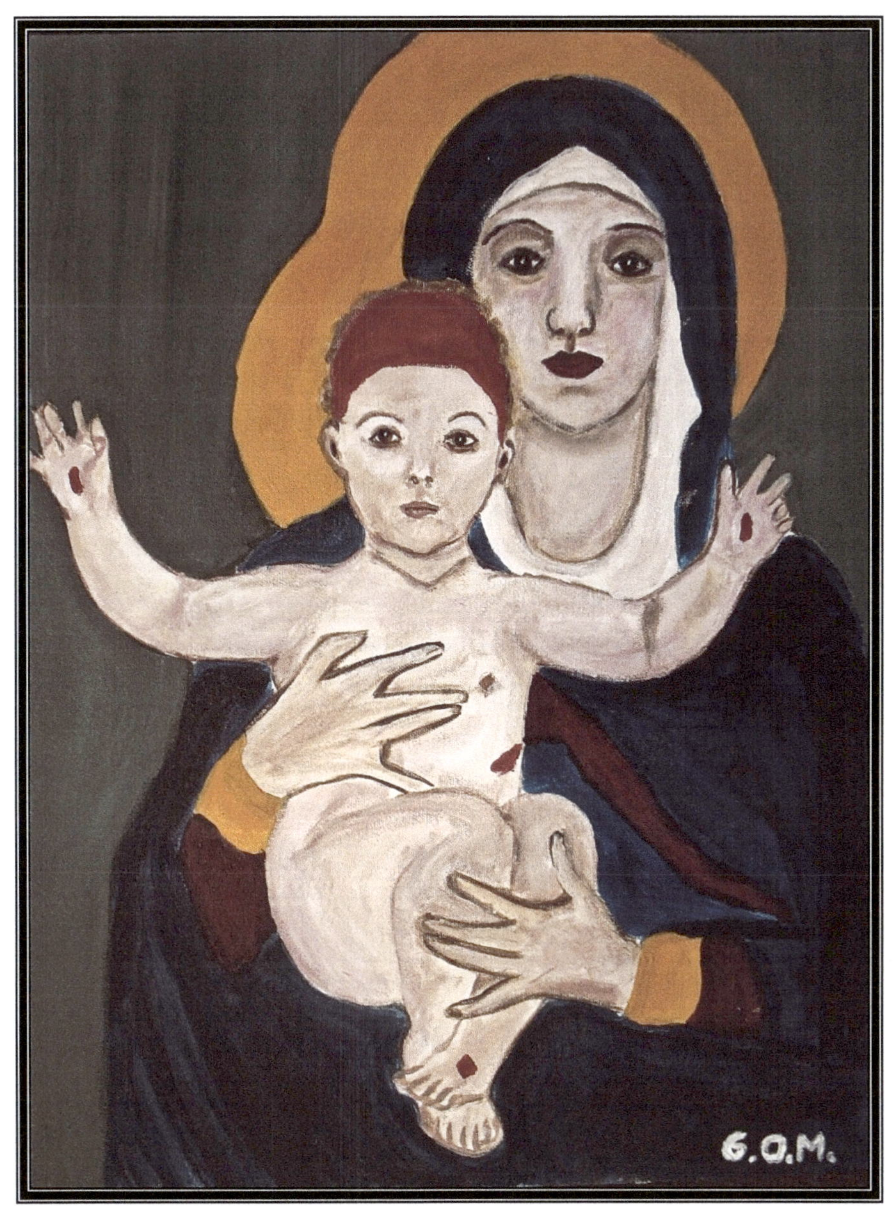

The Observer

"Though the Lord has given you the bread of suffering and water of distress, He who is your Teacher will hide no longer, but you will see your Teacher with your own eyes."

~ Isaiah 30:20

This is when my eyes began to see the Teacher that was present in this entire therapeutic journey. A Teacher resided in the wisdom and experience of Dr. A. A Teacher lived in my own heart's search for transformation. This is when I realized that all of life, God and my own being is the Teacher and the Taught, the Observer and the Observed.

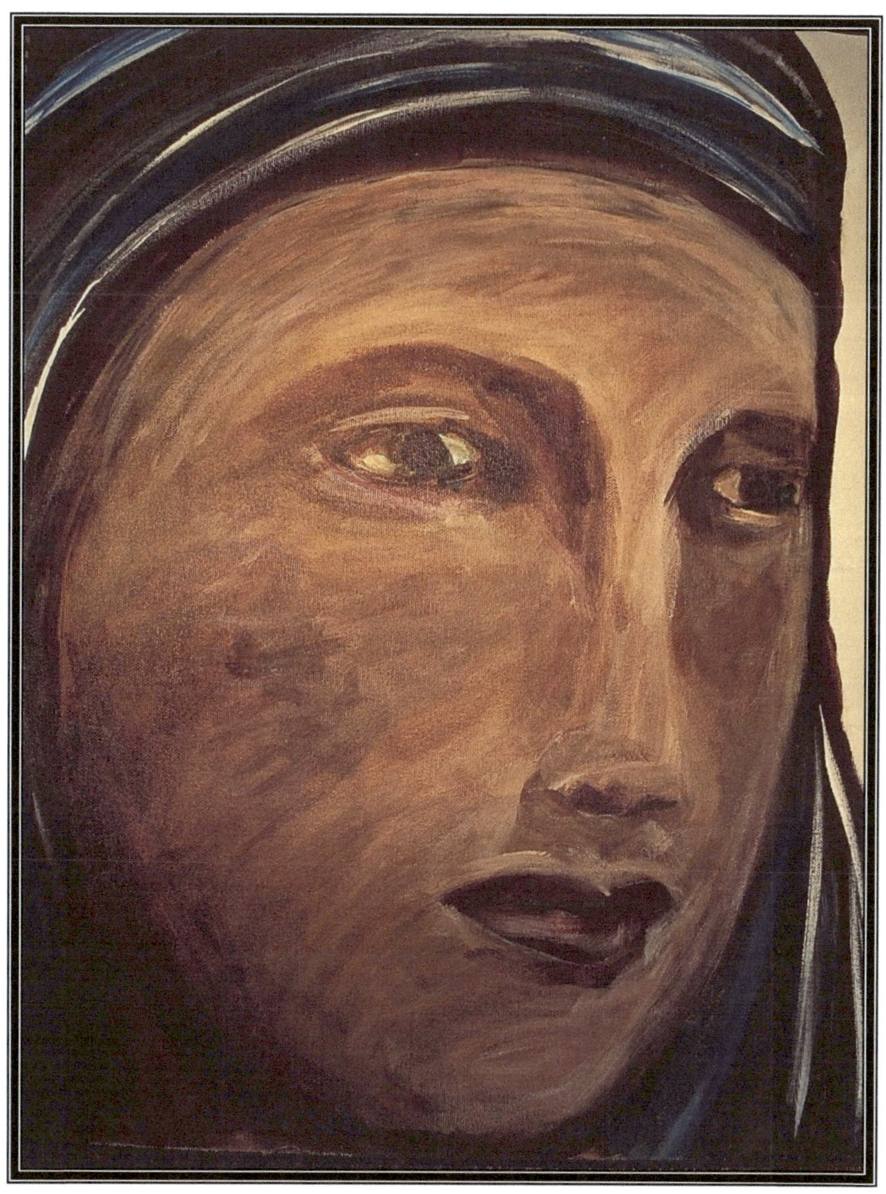

Self Portrait of a Soul

"Do not pray for tasks equal to your power. Pray for powers equal to your tasks. Then the doing of your work shall be no miracle, but you shall be the miracle."

~ Phillips Brooks

I chose the quote of Phillips Brooks to accompany this because the whole process of this healing work required so much more than I felt I had within me. The task of healing was monumental. I needed monumental power to do this inner work. It is true that I had become the miracle I had been praying for through the grace of God, a moment by moment exertion of intense courage, and the support of my Witness, Dr. A.

As time went by, I realized that this was really a self-portrait of my soul. It became the image that I chose to use as my logo and my signature painting.

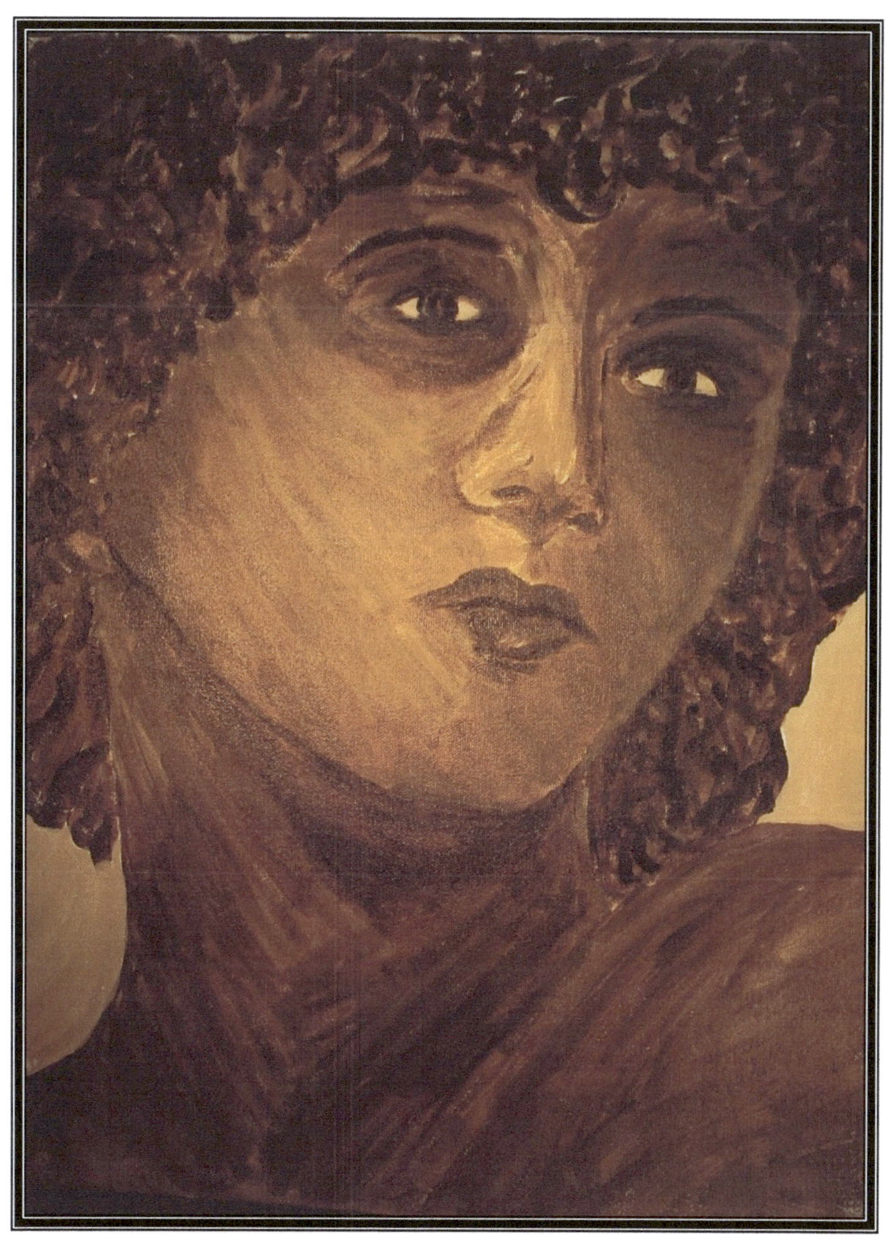

About the Author

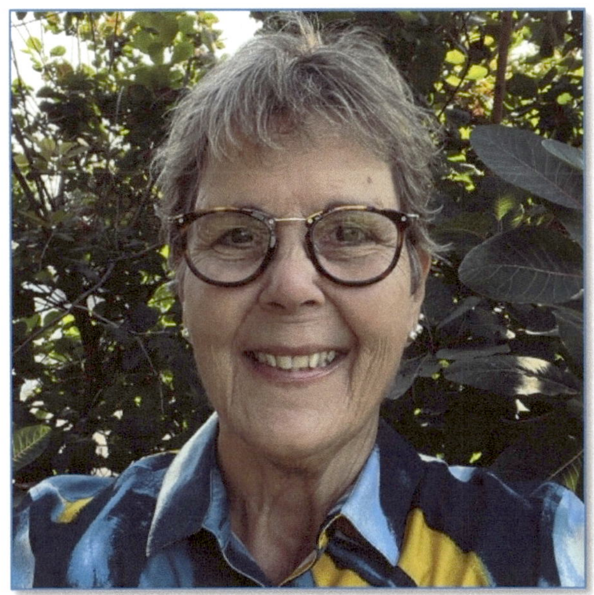

Veronica C. Wanchena is an author, artist and speaker in the field of trauma recovery. Having survived years of severe abuse and the debilitating consequences, she now stands joyfully as a beacon of light witnessing to the power of the human soul to heal.

Veronica used art as a primary tool of communication with her therapist Dr. A. and so recounts much of her story through the images she created. The depth of thorough healing she required called for enormous courage every step of the way. In her books, paintings and presentations, she eloquently offers a vivid and profound inside view of her survival strategies and healing process.

www.ingramcontent.com/pod-product-compliance
Lightning Source LLC
Chambersburg PA
CBHW042151030726
47599CB00004B/695